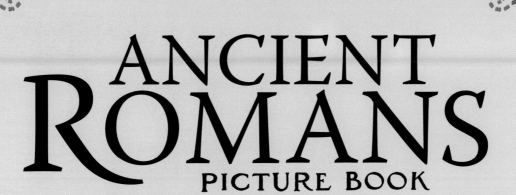

USBORNE
ANCIENT ROMANS
PICTURE BOOK

Megan Cullis
Illustrated by Wesley Robins

Designed by Samantha Barrett & Zuzanna Bukala
With thanks to Katharine Hoare at the British Museum

Contents

Dates

Some of the dates in this book are followed by
'BC', which stands for 'Before Christ'. This means
that the event happened before the birth of Jesus
Christ. This is supposed to have been over 2,000
years ago, in the year 1. BC dates are
counted backwards from this date.

THE ROMANS

The story of the ancient Romans started around 3,000 years ago, in Rome – at that time, a small city ruled by kings. Over several centuries, as the Romans gained power, Rome grew into the capital of a great empire, ruled by mighty emperors.

EARLY ROME

According to legend, Rome was founded in 753 BC by twin boys, Romulus and Remus. Romans believed they were sons of Mars, the god of war. Romulus became the first of a line of kings to rule Rome.

Legend has it that the twins were raised by a wolf. This statue shows Romulus and Remus as children suckling from the wolf.

Over the years, Rome grew into an impressive city. The Romans built a proper drainage system, a large public square and huge defensive walls to keep enemies out.

Some stories describe how Rome was saved from attack by a gaggle of cackling geese, warning that enemies were close.

The Romans were greatly influenced by the Etruscans – a powerful people in northern Italy. This sculpture was made by an Etruscan.

THE ROMAN REPUBLIC

In 510 BC, Rome became a republic run by the Senate – 300 men drawn from high-ranking Roman families. This lasted for nearly 500 years.

The Senate met regularly in the Senate House in Rome to discuss affairs of state.

A rare gold coin minted during Caesar's short time in power

THE END OF THE REPUBLIC

Then, in 44BC, an army general named Julius Caesar seized control of Rome, declaring himself a dictator, or sole ruler. The Roman republic was over, but Caesar's rule didn't last long – less than a year later, he was murdered.

BIRTH OF AN EMPIRE

After Caesar's death there was a great struggle for power. In 27 BC, Caesar's adopted son, Octavian, was granted supreme power after defeating his enemies in battle. He changed his name to Augustus, and became the first emperor to rule over the empire of Rome.

Augustus was a successful ruler. He built a new road network across the empire and developed an official courier system.

The emperor Augustus claimed he was related to the goddess Venus, who is symbolized by the little cupid at his side.

Over the next 400 years, there were all kinds of different emperors – some were fair and wise, others were power-hungry and cruel.

The emperor Claudius (41-54) was crippled by a disease. Most people thought he wasn't capable of ruling, but he turned out to be an excellent emperor.

The emperor Caligula (37-41) was thought to be insane. It is said that he fed his horse oats mixed with gold flakes, and even tried to make it a head of government.

Bronze sculpture of the emperor Claudius

Claudius was murdered in the year 54 – some people say his wife fed him poisoned mushrooms.

THE ROMAN ARMY

The Romans were able to conquer such a vast empire thanks to their mighty army. Well-trained and highly disciplined, it remained an unstoppable force for around three hundred years.

ORGANIZATION

There were two types of units in the army – legions and auxiliary units. A legion consisted of around 5,000 soldiers from Rome. An auxiliary unit contained up to 1,000 soldiers, mostly from outside Rome. Each unit was controlled by a number of senior soldiers.

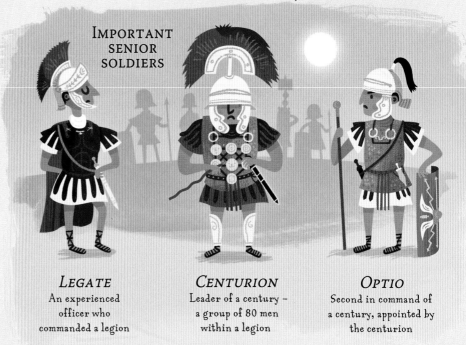

IMPORTANT SENIOR SOLDIERS

LEGATE
An experienced officer who commanded a legion

CENTURION
Leader of a century – a group of 80 men within a legion

OPTIO
Second in command of a century, appointed by the centurion

WEAPONS OF WAR

Some soldiers rode into battle on horseback, but most fought on foot, armed with javelins and swords. Sometimes they used heavier weapons, such as catapults.

This brass scabbard was used to protect a *gladius* – a type of short Roman sword. Many soldiers prided themselves on their flashy weapons.

This small dagger, called a *pugio*, dates from the year 150. It was hung from a soldier's belt.

This long sword, called a *spatha*, was used to thrust at the enemy. It was probably owned by a soldier who fought on horseback.

These soldiers are launching missiles from a catapult, or *ballista*. The Romans used different types of catapults. The most powerful could smash through walls.

DRESSING FOR BATTLE

Every soldier required strong protective gear that could withstand heavy blows. Types of gear changed over time, and differed between auxiliary and legionary soldiers.

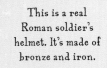

LEGIONARY

A legionary soldier received most of his uniform as standard issue. This soldier is wearing a helmet, breastplate, belt and sword.

AUXILIARY

Auxiliary soldiers wore gear typical of their individual regions. This soldier is wearing a chain mail tunic, with a helmet and leather belt.

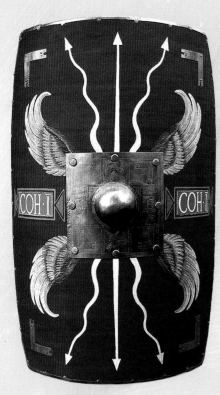

This is a real Roman soldier's helmet. It's made of bronze and iron.

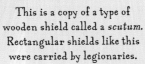

Each soldier wore a protective belt around his waist, hung with strips of leather studded with metal.

This is a copy of a type of wooden shield called a *scutum*. Rectangular shields like this were carried by legionaries.

This is a replica of a military sandal, made from strips of leather. Soldiers lined their sandals with wool to keep warm in winter.

THE CITY OF ROME

Capital of the empire and home to around one million people, Rome became the largest city in the ancient world. Magnificent public buildings lined the streets, alongside crowded apartment blocks, shops and markets.

At the heart of the city of Rome was a large, open space called the Forum. This is how it would have looked around the year 400.

GRAND DESIGNS

Rome was full of impressive monuments and buildings, some of which still stand today. Many were commissioned by emperors who wanted to leave their mark on the city's landscape.

Trajan's Column was built to commemorate a war victory by the emperor Trajan.

The Arch of Constantine was built in the year 315 to celebrate a battle victory.

One of the most famous buildings in Rome is the Colosseum – a vast stone stadium that stands in partial ruins today.

Each gleaming marble or vast stone structure boasted of the glory of Rome. The emperor Augustus claimed he had found Rome a city of bricks and left it a city of marble.

CITY WALLS

The city of Rome sprawled across seven hills on the banks of the Tiber river. Such a vast city was vulnerable to attack, so the Romans built high defensive walls to keep enemies out.

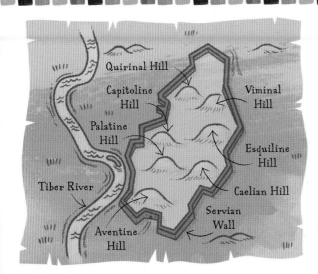

Quirinal Hill
Capitoline Hill
Viminal Hill
Palatine Hill
Esquiline Hill
Tiber River
Caelian Hill
Servian Wall
Aventine Hill

This map shows the seven hills of Rome. The original city wall, the Servian Wall, was built between 377 and 353 BC.

DAILY LIFE

Despite its glamorous appearance, Rome was very overcrowded. Most people lived in cramped apartment blocks, called *insulae*, which could be up to seven floors high.

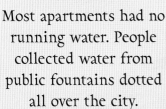

Roman insulae were often poorly built, and were vulnerable to fire and collapse.

Most apartments had no running water. People collected water from public fountains dotted all over the city.

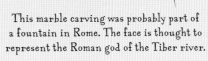

This marble carving was probably part of a fountain in Rome. The face is thought to represent the Roman god of the Tiber river.

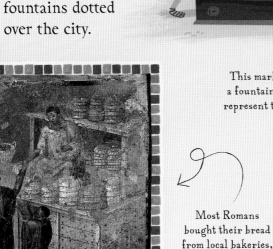

Most Romans bought their bread from local bakeries, like this one.

Those who lived in insulae were not allowed their own ovens, due to the risk of fire. They bought food from local food stalls, or snacked in taverns and bars.

A ROMAN HOUSE

Most wealthy Romans owned a grand house in town, called a *domus*. Large, airy, and beautifully furnished, a domus served as a family home and a place to receive guests.

INSIDE A DOMUS

This very grand domus has a kitchen, a dining room, a study, some bedrooms and a bathroom. All the rooms are arranged around a central hall, called an *atrium*, where guests were received.

Most atriums had a shrine like this. The family left offerings for household gods beneath the shrine.

WALLS AND FLOORS

Walls inside houses were covered with paintings. Floors were often laid with mosaics – patterns or scenes made from thousands of small cut stones.

BEDROOM

STUDY

SHOP

SHRIN.

POOL

ATRIUM

The rooms at the front of the house were rented out as shops.

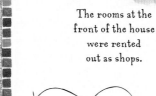

This mosaic shows a fierce dog. It was laid at the entrance of a house to warn off intruders.

THE GARDEN

A garden was usually at the back of the house, surrounded by a covered walkway. Flowers and trees grew there and fountains cooled the air.

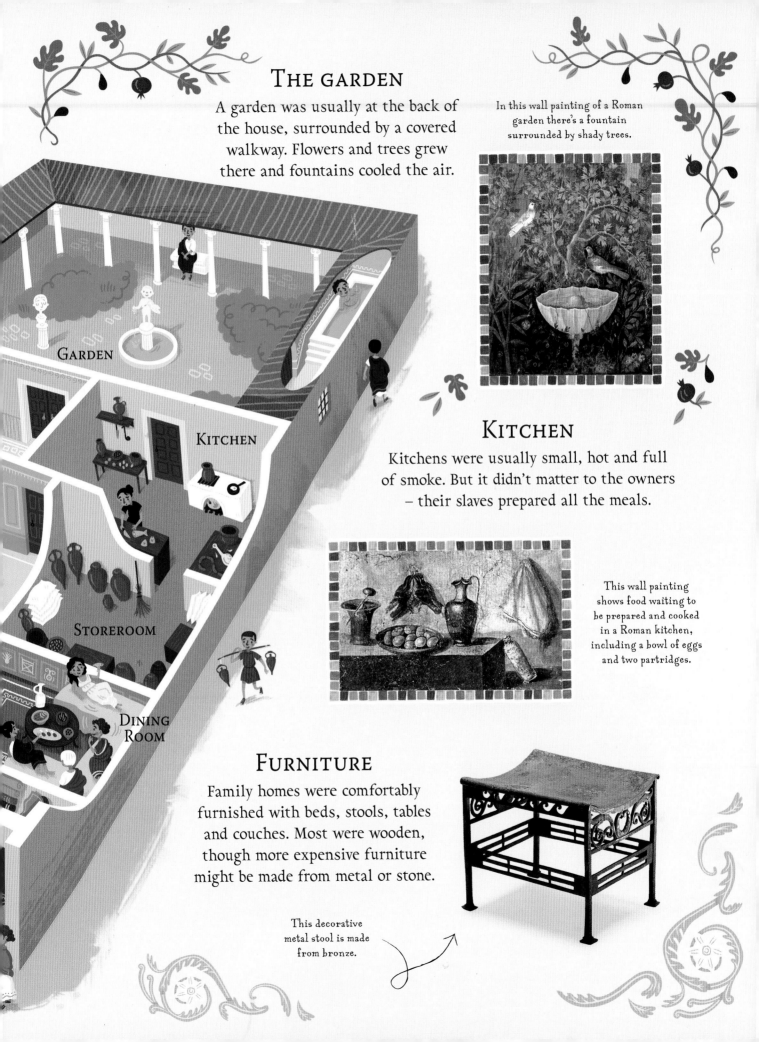

In this wall painting of a Roman garden there's a fountain surrounded by shady trees.

GARDEN

KITCHEN

STOREROOM

DINING ROOM

KITCHEN

Kitchens were usually small, hot and full of smoke. But it didn't matter to the owners – their slaves prepared all the meals.

This wall painting shows food waiting to be prepared and cooked in a Roman kitchen, including a bowl of eggs and two partridges.

FURNITURE

Family homes were comfortably furnished with beds, stools, tables and couches. Most were wooden, though more expensive furniture might be made from metal or stone.

This decorative metal stool is made from bronze.

ARTS AND CRAFTS

Rome was packed with craft workshops busy producing all kinds of different wares, from glistening gold necklaces to fancy dishes and vases.

GLASS

The Romans became very skilled at working with glass. They made jugs, bowls and vases by blowing melted glass into bubbles and shaping the glass in containers as it cooled.

The sparkling bowl above is made from ribbons of bright glass, decorated with real gold.

This vase was made by blowing blue glass with a layer of white glass on the outside. Some of the white glass was then cut away to create the scene.

Glass workers blew air through long metal pipes to shape the molten glass.

POTTERY

Pottery was a huge industry in ancient Rome. Pottery jars, called *amphorae*, were produced in their millions to store wine and oil. Smaller, more decorative pots were crafted by specialized potters.

This ornate pottery flask is in the shape of a chicken. It would have been used for pouring wine.

Amphorae were loaded into trade ships and transported across the empire.

METAL

Some workshops echoed with the sounds of crashing and banging, as metalworkers hammered tools, knives, pots and pans from copper, iron and bronze.

This marble relief shows a copper workshop, where craftworkers are hammering and weighing out metal.

This metalworker is hammering a piece of red hot iron on a metal block, called an anvil. He's shaping the iron into a knife blade.

Goldsmiths and silversmiths produced necklaces, rings and ornaments decorated with elaborate designs.

This striking necklace is made of gold and set with emeralds and large pearls, called 'blister' pearls.

Detailed mosaics, like this one, would have been arranged in a workshop before being transported and laid in place.

MAKING MOSAICS

Skilled craftworkers made tiled patterns or scenes, called mosaics, to decorate the walls or floors of buildings. Mosaics were made from tiny cubes called *tesserae* that were cut from stone, marble, pottery or glass.

Craftworkers pressed tesserae into wet cement to create a mosaic.

COUNTRY LIFE

The Roman empire is famous for its cities, but most people lived in the country. Many worked on farms for wealthy landowners, who visited their country estates to relax and entertain in comfortable country houses.

ON THE FARM

Italy's hot, sunny climate was perfect for farming all kinds of crops. Wheat was grown to make bread, while vast quantities of grapes and olives were cultivated to make wine and oil.

This wall painting shows some types of fruit that were grown on farms, including apples, grapes and pomegranates.

Pigeons were kept in a dovecote, for their meat and eggs.

Country house

Oxen pulled metal tools to dig up the fields.

Vegetable patch

Grain store

Beehives for honey

Vineyards

This mosaic shows farm workers treading grapes with their feet to extract the juice for making wine.

Out in the olive groves, many workers spent hours harvesting olives, before pressing them to make oil.

Wine and olive oil were stored in pottery jars, like this one, called *amphorae*.

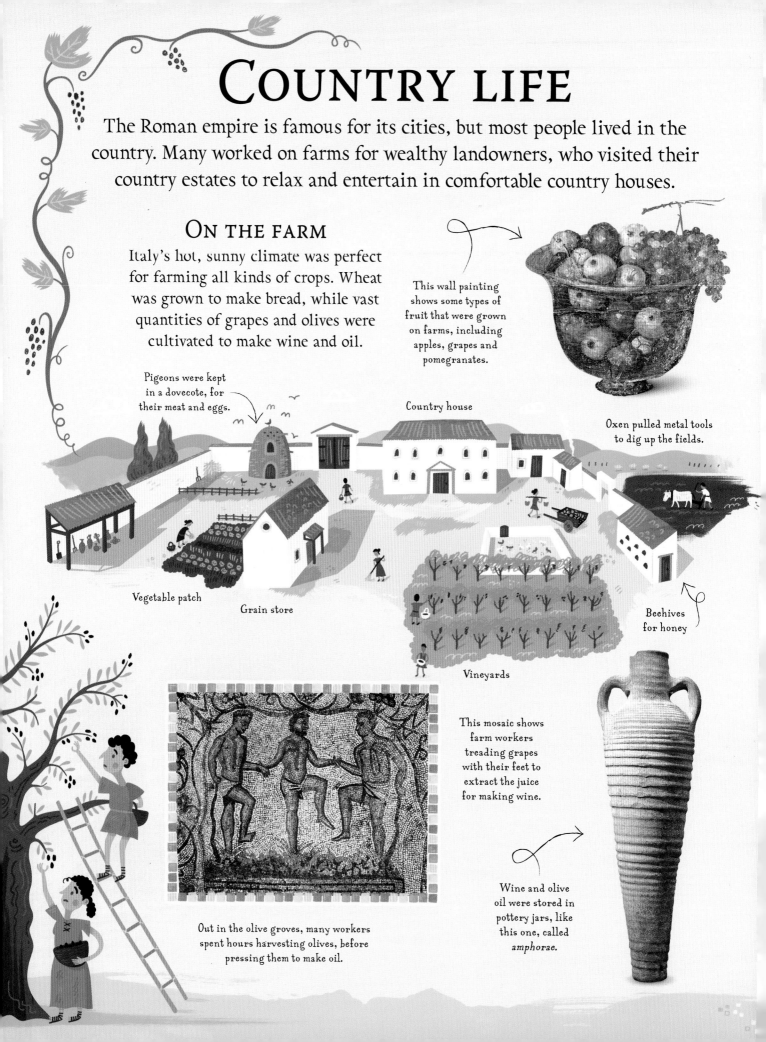

HUNTING

The countryside provided plenty of opportunities to hunt wild animals. People hunted to provide food for their families, and the wealthy hunted as a sociable pastime, too.

In this mosaic of a hunting party, one of the hunters is directing his dogs to chase a boar into a net. Other hunters are carrying a dead boar home.

DINNER PARTIES

Wealthy Romans hosted lavish dinner parties, called *cenae*, inside their country houses. Tables were laid with all kinds of exotic delicacies, from dormice and pigeons to flamingo tongues and even elephant trunks.

This silver drinking cup was used for wine.

Luxury glassware, like this ornate bottle, was displayed to show off the wealth of the host.

These Romans have gathered together for a cena.

A servant brings in more wine.

Diners recline on wide couches.

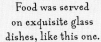

Food was served on exquisite glass dishes, like this one.

GROWING UP

In Roman times, children had very different experiences of growing up, depending on their backgrounds. For example, only children from wealthy families went to school.

STARTING LIFE

At eight or nine days old, every baby was named during a formal ceremony, and given a lucky charm, which was meant to ward off evil spirits.

This gold charm, called a *bulla*, belonged to a boy. He wore it around his neck.

WORK OR PLAY

Children born into rich families had lots of toys to play with, from rattles filled with stones to wooden swords and dolls.

Those from poorer families had little time to play. They started working at an early age around the house, in a workshop or on the land.

This child slave, taken from a large mosaic, is carrying a plate of figs and a bucket of fish.

These toys once belonged to Roman children. The doll is wooden and the marbles are made from glass.

OFF TO SCHOOL

From age six until eleven, wealthy girls and boys went to a *ludus*, or elementary school. After that, boys continued their studies at secondary school, or *grammaticus*. Some girls and boys were also taught by private tutors at home.

At a ludus, pupils sat on low stools in front of their teacher.

READING AND WRITING

At school, children learned to read and write in Latin – the Roman language that was spoken across the empire. They wrote on wooden tablets covered in a thick layer of wax, scratching their letters with a pointed stick, called a *stylus*.

This wall painting shows a girl holding a wooden tablet and stylus.

These are real Roman styluses. Their ends are flat for smoothing out scratches in the wax, a little like an eraser.

LATIN PHRASES

Although Latin isn't spoken as a first language any more, many Latin words and phrases are still in use today.

Status quo Existing state of affairs
Vice versa The other way around
Et cetera And the rest (or etc.)

Pupils were mainly assessed on their oral skills, and were trained in public speaking.

INTO ADULTHOOD

Girls and boys were recognized as adults at around the age of 14. A boy was presented with adult clothes as a sign that he was grown up. Girls were expected to marry and have children of their own.

These gold Roman wedding rings show couples clasping hands – a symbol of marriage.

Most weddings were held in June, which was considered a lucky month.

FASHION AND BEAUTY

Rich Roman men and women spent time on their appearance, from grooming their hair to adorning themselves with perfumes and glistening jewels.

GETTING DRESSED

Clothes were a way of showing a person's status. Most people wore simple knee-length tunics, while wealthy Romans added more elaborate layers on top.

EVERYDAY CLOTHING

A woman wore a long robe called a *stola*. She draped a shawl, called a *palla*, over her shoulder.

Glass mirrors hadn't been invented, so Romans used highly polished metal mirrors. Many had decorated backs, like this one.

A wealthy man wore a *toga* – a semicircular piece of wool cloth folded around his body.

SMELLING SWEET

Perfumes were worn by both men and women. They were made using flowers, herbs or spices and mixed with animal fats and oil.

Decorative glass bottles, like these, were used to store perfume.

This wall painting shows a woman pouring perfume into a bottle.

Rose and iris were two of the most popular scents.

HAIR AND MAKEUP

Rich women wore elaborate hairstyles and makeup, just as people do today. Fancy updos took many hours to perfect, but there were usually slaves to help.

This sculpture shows a Roman woman with a hairstyle of elaborately arranged curls. False hairpieces were used to give these hairstyles extra volume.

Women used a natural red powder to rouge their cheeks, and powdered chalk to whiten their faces.

Combs, like this ivory one, were used to de-tangle hair and get rid of lice.

ORNAMENTS

Jewels were worn by both men and women. Rich men wore rings engraved with designs known as seals, which could be stamped into wax. They were used to authenticate documents, like a signature. Women wore a glittering array of bracelets, necklaces and earrings.

This ornate gold necklace is made from coins showing the faces of different emperors.

This gold armband is shaped like a snake. For the Romans, snakes were symbols of healing and protection.

These delicate earrings are made from polished emeralds threaded onto gold wire.

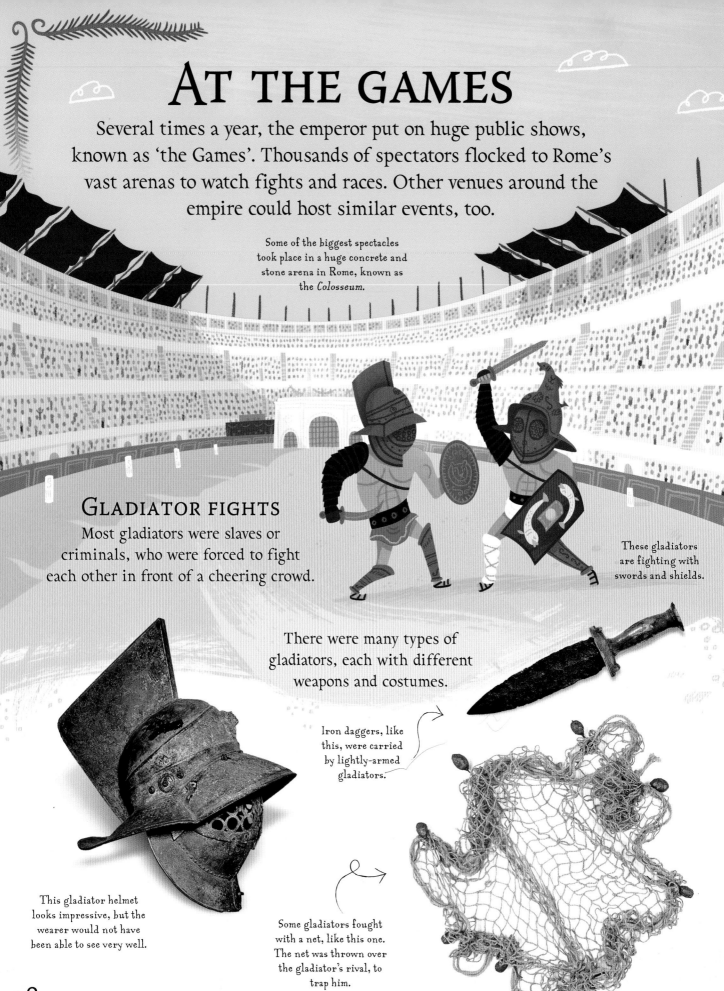

AT THE GAMES

Several times a year, the emperor put on huge public shows, known as 'the Games'. Thousands of spectators flocked to Rome's vast arenas to watch fights and races. Other venues around the empire could host similar events, too.

Some of the biggest spectacles took place in a huge concrete and stone arena in Rome, known as the *Colosseum*.

GLADIATOR FIGHTS

Most gladiators were slaves or criminals, who were forced to fight each other in front of a cheering crowd.

These gladiators are fighting with swords and shields.

There were many types of gladiators, each with different weapons and costumes.

Iron daggers, like this, were carried by lightly-armed gladiators.

This gladiator helmet looks impressive, but the wearer would not have been able to see very well.

Some gladiators fought with a net, like this one. The net was thrown over the gladiator's rival, to trap him.

18

FAME AND FORTUNE

Victorious gladiators were adored by their fans. They usually received prize money and a palm leaf of victory. Slave gladiators could even win their freedom.

The winning gladiator often ran a victory lap around the arena.

BATTLE OF THE BEASTS

Wild animal hunts were also popular arena shows. Exotic creatures, such as elephants and tigers, were pitted against each other or were hunted down with spears and daggers.

This mosaic shows a bloody fight between an armed gladiator and a ferocious leopard.

CHARIOT RACING

Chariot races were held inside specially built stadiums. Around 250,000 could fit into the largest stadiums, to watch as up to twelve chariots thundered around the track.

The chariot racing track in Rome was known as the *Circus Maximus*. Chariots raced around a central barrier decorated with elaborate pillars and statues.

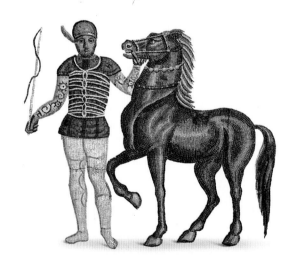

This detail from a mosaic shows a charioteer wearing a green tunic. Charioteers competed in four main teams – Green, Red, Blue and White.

This bronze model shows a two-horse chariot, but one horse has been lost. A chariot could be pulled by up to eight horses – the more horses there were, the more skill was needed to control the chariot.

19

ENTERTAINMENT

As well as gladiator fights and chariot racing, the Romans had other forms of entertainment too, from watching plays and concerts to relaxing in public baths.

PLAYS

The Romans put on two main types of plays. 'Tragedies' were sad plays about gods and heroes. 'Comedies' were funny, lighthearted plays about ordinary people. All the actors wore masks.

The mosaic above shows a group of actors getting ready to perform a play. Female characters were played by men – women weren't allowed to act.

This mosaic shows two acting masks – one is a character from a tragedy (left), and the other is from a comedy (right).

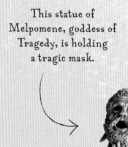

This statue of Melpomene, goddess of Tragedy, is holding a tragic mask.

At first, plays were staged in temporary wooden buildings. Later, permanent stone playhouses were built, some seating thousands of people.

Roman plays were noisy affairs. The audience often shouted and jeered at the actors during a performance.

MAKING MUSIC

Music was played during festivals, religious ceremonies and other social occasions. Musicians also played and sang during performances of some plays.

Roman musical instruments were not too different from those played today.

Long bronze trumpet, or *tuba*

Bronze horn, called a *cornu*

Stringed instrument, called a *lyre*

Organ, known as a *hydraulis*

This mosaic shows a scene from a play. Musicians in masks are playing a tambourine, a pair of tiny cymbals and a double flute.

AT THE BATHS

Most people didn't have bathrooms at home, so public baths were always bustling with activity. Most Romans visited their local baths every day to wash and pamper themselves. Women and men usually had separate bathhouses, or bathed at different times.

To clean themselves, people rubbed perfumed oil into their skin. It was kept in a flask like this and a metal tool, or *strigil*, was used to scrape it off, taking the dirt with it.

Most public bathhouses contained a mixture of warm and hot baths and cold plunge pools.

Games, such as dice throwing, were played at the edge of the pool.

GODS AND GODDESSES

The Romans believed in hundreds of different gods and goddesses. Each one ruled a different aspect of life. Here are some of the most important ones.

JUNO

Juno was the goddess of women and marriage. She was married to Jupiter, the king of the gods, and is often pictured with a peacock.

JUPITER

Jupiter was king of the gods, ruler of the skies and god of thunder and lightning. He sometimes took the shape of an eagle.

VENUS

Venus was the goddess of love and beauty. She was believed to have emerged from the waves fully grown and standing on a seashell. She was married to the god Vulcan.

VULCAN

Vulcan was god of craftworkers and destructive fires. His fiery forge was believed to be located under Mount Etna, on the island of Sicily.

MARS

The Romans held festivals for Mars, god of war, every year. The month of March (*Martius* in Latin) is named after him.

VESTA

Goddess of the hearth, home and family. Her symbol was a sacred fire.

NEPTUNE

Neptune was god of the sea, earthquakes and horses. He was usually shown holding a weapon known as a trident.

CERES

Ceres was the goddess of agriculture and fertility. The Romans held many festivals for Ceres, including a week-long celebration during harvest time.

PLUTO

Feared by all, Pluto was god of the underworld. He was accompanied by a three-headed dog, called Cerberus.

DIANA

Diana was goddess of the moon and hunting. She was often shown with deer, holding a bow and arrow. Diana was the twin sister of the god Apollo.

MERCURY

Mercury was god of travel. He served as Jupiter's messenger, and had wings on his shoes and hat.

MINERVA

Goddess of crafts and war, Minerva was usually accompanied by an owl, to symbolize her wisdom.

APOLLO

God of the sun, music, healing and prophecy, Apollo was also the bringer of ill-health and plague.

BACCHUS

Owner of an ivy-covered staff dripping with honey, Bacchus was the god of wine and merrymaking.

23

POMPEII

Pompeii is now one of the most famous cities of the Roman world. Nestled into the foothills of Mount Vesuvius in southern Italy, it was just an ordinary Roman city, until one day, in the year 79, disaster struck...

ERUPTION!

Mount Vesuvius – a volcano that had been quiet for hundreds of years – suddenly exploded. A cloud of hot gases and rocks rolled down into Pompeii, killing everyone in its path.

Later, ash covered the dead. The bodies gradually decayed, leaving holes in the ash. Centuries later, plaster was poured into the holes, revealing shapes like this man and dog.

A BLANKET OF ASH

On the second day, a thick cloud of ash and pumice settled over the wreckage of the city. Over the following weeks, it turned hard as stone. Pompeii lay entombed in 6m (20ft) of solid ash and pumice for the next 1,700 years.

Clouds of ash rained down on Pompeii, smothering every building in the city.

Even Pompeii's great stone stadium, shown in this wall painting, was completely buried.

Discovery

It wasn't until 1748 that people dug through the ash and the city's ruins were finally discovered. The absence of air and moisture under the ash meant that everything had been almost perfectly preserved.

King Charles III of Spain, who ruled this part of Italy at the time, ordered the first excavations. Many of the finds were added to his art collection.

Even the most delicate wall paintings were found intact. This painting shows women dancing to celebrate the god Bacchus.

Lost treasures

From mosaics, paintings and jewels to everyday objects like pottery and even food, all kinds of objects survived the eruption. No other Roman site has revealed such rich evidence of Roman life.

This loaf of bread was found in a bakery. It had been cut into slices, ready to eat.

A bowl of eggs from a kitchen in Pompeii were even recovered with some of the shells unbroken.

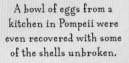

These bowls were discovered full of bright powder, which would have been used to make wall paintings.

This picture shows how Pompeii looks today. All these buildings were revealed by digging down very carefully and removing all the ash.

MASTER BUILDERS

Across their empire, the Romans erected magnificent buildings, bridges and other impressive structures. At first they copied Greek styles, but gradually they developed their own distinctive designs.

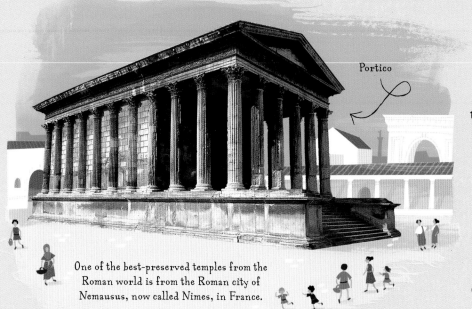

Portico

TEMPLES

Inspired by Greek temples, the Romans built rectangular ones with an outer row of columns supporting the roof. A grand porch, called a *portico*, emphasized the front of the building.

One of the best-preserved temples from the Roman world is from the Roman city of Nemausus, now called Nimes, in France.

COLUMNS

The Romans used five types of columns, each with different tops, known as capitals. Below you can see the different styles.

ARCHES

Arches were a feature of many Roman buildings. Buildings were often formed of many different-sized arches, joining each other at various heights and angles.

The Basilica Maxentius in Rome was entirely constructed from arches.

COMPOSITE

CORINTHIAN

IONIC

TUSCAN

DORIC

DOMES

One of the Romans' greatest innovations was the invention of the dome. They achieved this by crossing several arches over one another.

Towering over ancient Rome, this domed building, called the Pantheon, was probably built as a temple. Its dome was the largest in the ancient world.

The Pantheon survives to this day. This 300-year-old painting shows the inside of the dome, which is made of concrete – another Roman invention.

VIADUCTS AND AQUEDUCTS

The Romans also used arches to build incredible layered bridges, called *aqueducts* and *viaducts*. Viaducts carried roads high above the ground, while aqueducts carried water in raised channels.

This is an aqueduct. Water flowed along a channel at the top.

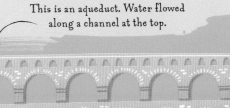

ROADS

The Roman empire was connected by thousands of miles of roads. They were built as straight as possible. This made them quicker and easier to use, but much harder to build.

Roman surveyors used an instrument called a *groma* to work out the straightest route.

Groma

THE FALL OF ROME

For 200 years, the Roman empire seemed unbeatable.
But by around the year 230, it was showing signs of strain.
After many years of conflict, the empire finally collapsed,
changing the Roman way of life forever.

TROUBLED TIMES

Invasions, money troubles and a terrible plague had
made the empire more and more difficult to control.
In the year 285, the emperor Diocletian divided it in
two. He ruled the eastern half, and gave command of
the western half to an army general named Maximian.

This carving shows
Diocletian and Maximian
wearing gold coronets
in the shape of laurel
wreaths, to show their
shared power.

Diocletian clung on to
many old Roman traditions,
insisting on elaborate
ceremonies to demonstrate
his power as emperor.

A NEW CAPITAL

Soon after Diocletian and Maximian retired,
an army general named Constantine took control of
the west. He reunited the empire, eventually becoming
sole emperor. He also moved the capital from Rome to
Byzantium (now called Istanbul), and renamed
it Constantinople, after himself.

Constantine had a colossal
bronze and marble statue
of himself built in Rome to
remind people of his power.

This glittering mosaic, made
around the year 1000, shows
Constantine holding the city of
Constantinople in his hands.

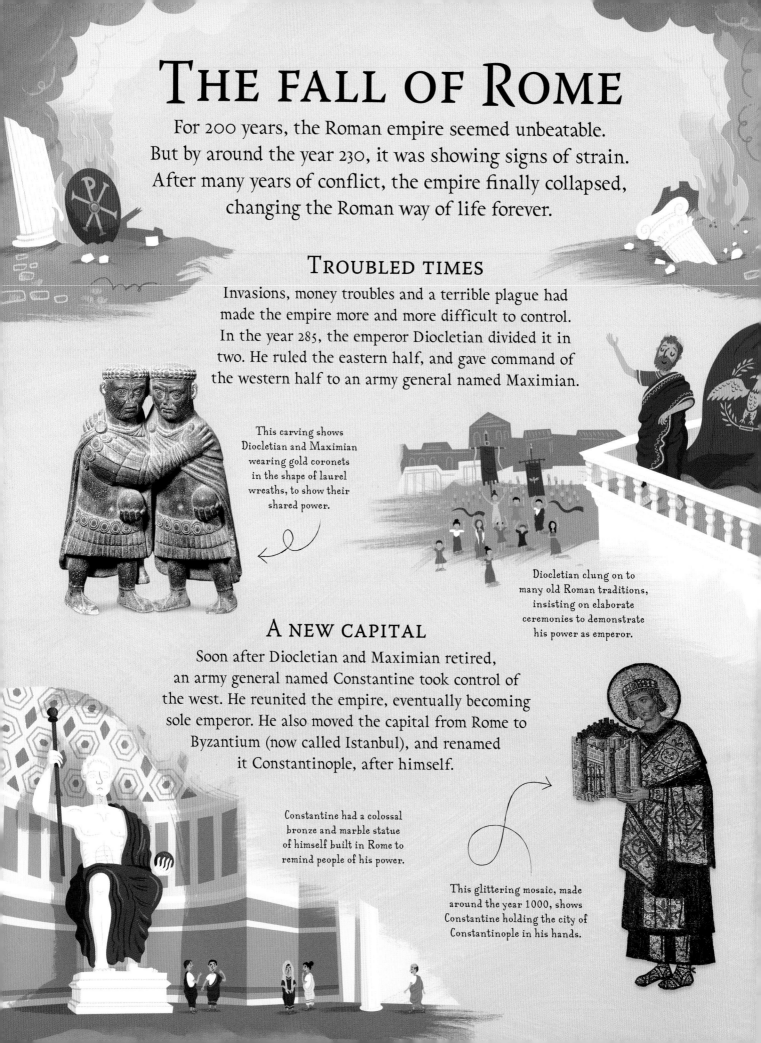

THE RISE OF CHRISTIANITY

Under Constantine's rule, the Christian religion flourished. By the year 391 it had grown so popular that Constantine declared it the empire's official religion. Before Constantine, Christians were persecuted because they refused to follow the Roman religion.

In the reigns of some emperors, Christians were publically tormented. This mosaic shows a Christian being attacked by lions.

Before long, the leaders of the Christian Church had grown very powerful. Their head, known as the Pope, became almost as powerful as the emperor.

It is said that before he came to power, Constantine saw a cross of light in the sky, which he believed was a sign from Christ.

This jewel-encrusted golden cross was made around the year 570 and owned by an early pope.

THE END OF THE EMPIRE

In the year 395, the empire split again. The western half, ruled from Rome, was overrun by tribes from outside, and finally collapsed in 476.

In 410, Visigoths attacked the city of Rome, and burned much of it to the ground.

This eagle brooch was made by a people known as the Visigoths, who lived beyond the empire, but began to settle in Roman lands.

The eastern empire, ruled from Constantinople, lasted for a thousand years longer than the western empire. Today, the Romans are just memories, but their buildings, laws and art, and their astonishing empire, still have the power to amaze people.

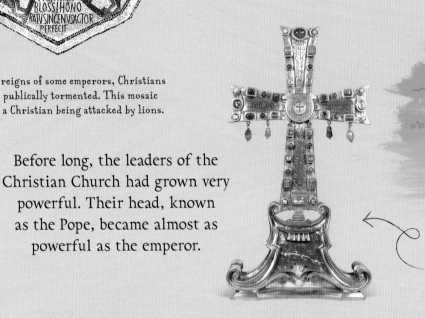

THE ROMAN EMPIRE

This map shows the Roman empire around the year 116 when it was at its peak, stretching across Europe, North Africa and parts of the Middle East. Thousands of miles of roads linked Rome to every corner of the empire.

In the year 43, the Romans invaded *Britannia*. They conquered most of England and Wales, but struggled to capture Scotland. In 117, the emperor Hadrian had a huge wall built to keep out the northern tribes.

Hadrian's wall

BRITANNIA

Beyond the empire in *Germania*, fierce tribes opposed the Romans. The Romans saw them as inferior, and called them 'barbarians'.

GERMANIA

After the victory at Alesia, the Gallic general surrendered his weapons and was taken back to Rome as a prisoner.

Gallia (most of modern-day France) fell to the Romans in 52 BC, at the Battle of Alesia, where a Roman general named Julius Caesar defeated the ruling Gallic tribes.

ALESIA

ILLYRICUM

GALLIA

The city of *Roma* (Rome) was the capital of the mighty empire. A vast network of roads ran out from it.

ROMA

POMPEII

In 218 BC, a general from Carthage, named Hannibal, set off from Spain with an army of 100,000 men and 38 elephants to attack the Romans in Italy.

Hispania was conquered in around 19 BC. The Roman emperors Trajan, Hadrian and Marcus Aurelius were all born here.

Gold coin of Hadrian

TARRACO

Mount Vesuvius, near Pompeii, erupted in the year 79, burying the city.

ITALIA

HISPANIA

CORDOBA

The Roman army sailed across the Mediterranean Sea on warships, called *quadriremes*.

CARTHAGE

Carthage was the home of the Carthaginians, powerful rivals of the Romans. After three great wars, the Romans finally conquered Carthage in 146 BC.

KEY

- ● CITY
- ～ RIVER
- ▢ ROMAN TERRITORY

Place names on this map are shown in Latin – the language of the Romans.

N
W   E
S

Byzantium was an important fishing port until the year 330, when the emperor Constantine made it the new capital of the Roman empire and renamed it Constantinople.

The Romans traded silk, spices and perfumes in lands beyond the empire, including parts of modern Asia and China. Goods were transported across the desert on packs of camels.

Antioch, conquered by the Roman general Pompey in 64 BC, became the third largest city in the empire, after Rome and Alexandria. It was nicknamed the 'Queen of the East'.

● **BYZANTIUM**

ASIA

ANTIOCH ●

SYRIA

● **PERGAMUM**

Ancient Pergamum

In 133 BC, the Romans took control of the area they called *Asia*, after Attalus III, the King of Pergamum, left his kingdom to the Romans in his will.

Pompey proved such an excellent general that his troops called him Pompey the Great.

MEDITERRANEAN SEA

Aegyptus (now Egypt) was conquered by the Romans in 30 BC. The area was very valuable due to its rich supply of grain and papyrus – a type of plant used to make paper.

Gerasa (now Jerash, in Jordan) became part of the Roman empire in 63 BC. It was an important trading city, and the emperor Hadrian even visited it from Rome.

GERASA ●

This arch was built in Gerasa to celebrate Hadrian's visit.

○ **ALEXANDRIA**

ARABIA

AEGYPTUS

When the Egyptian queen, Cleopatra, heard of the Romans' victory, she killed herself, supposedly by getting a snake to bite her.

The Arabian desert was populated by nomadic people, who became allies of the Romans.

INDEX

Usborne Quicklinks

For links to websites where you can see reconstructions of ancient Rome, take virtual tours of the ruins and discover more about life in Roman times, go to the Usborne Quicklinks website at **www.usborne.com/quicklinks** and type in the keywords 'Ancient Romans picture book'. Please read our internet safety guidelines at the Usborne Quicklinks website.

Acknowledgements

Every effort has been made to trace and acknowledge ownership of copyright. If any rights have been omitted, the publishers offer to rectify this in any future editions following notification. The publishers are grateful to the following individuals and organizations for their permission to reproduce material on the following pages:
(t=top, m=middle, b=bottom, r=right, l=left)

COVER: bl © Iberfoto / Iberfoto / Superstock; mr © Heritage Image Partnership Ltd / Alamy; br © The Art Archive / Archaeological Museum Naples / Araldo De Luca.

PAGES 2-3 The Romans: p2 t © Nevena Tsvetanova / Alamy; p2 m © Werner Forman Archive / Private Collection Location 14; p3 t © Rare Ancient Roman Coin, Roman Gold Aureus, Julius Caesar, c 43 BC, minted in Cisalpine Gaul (photo) / Hoberman/UIG / Bridgeman Images; p3 m © Augustus of Prima Porta, c.20 BC (marble), Roman, (1st century BC) / Vatican Museums and Galleries, Vatican City / Bridgeman Images; p3 b © The Trustees of the British Museum.

PAGES 4-5 The Roman army: p4 bl © INTERFOTO / Alamy; p4 bm © The Trustees of the British Museum; p4 br © Museum of London; p5 t © The Trustees of the British Museum; p5 m, bl and br - photos courtesy of Matt Lukes of FABRICA ROMANORVM Recreations.

PAGES 6-7 The city of Rome: p6 bl © Independent Picture Service / Alamy; p6 bm and br © Photo Scala, Florence - courtesy of the Ministero Beni e Att. Culturali; p7 m © Werner Forman Archive; p7 b © Photo Scala, Florence/Fotografica Foglia - courtesy of the Ministero Beni e Att. Culturali.

PAGES 8-9 A Roman house: p8 t © Household shrine, from the Casa dei Vetti (House of the Vettii) (fresco on stone), Roman, (1st century BC) / Pompeii, Italy / Bridgeman Images; p8 b © Dog on a leash, from Pompeii (mosaic), Roman, (1st century AD) / Museo Archeologico Nazionale, Naples, Italy / Giraudon / Bridgeman Images; p9 t © Detail of fountain and birds from a garden painting, House of the Golden Bracelet, Pompeii / De Agostini Picture Library / L. Pedicini / Bridgeman Images; p9 m © Wall Painting of a Kitchen, House of Julia Felix, Pompeii, Italy, 2007 (wall painting), Roman, (1st century AD) / Pompeii, Italy / © Samuel Magal, Sites & Photos Ltd. / Bridgeman Images; p9 b © The Trustees of the British Museum.

PAGES 10-11 Arts and crafts: p10 tl © The Trustees of the British Museum; p10 tr © James L. Amos/Corbis; p10 b and p11 t © DeAgostini / DeAgostini / Superstock; p11 m © The Art Archive / Alamy; p11 b © Christie's Images Ltd. / Christie's Images Ltd./ Superstock.

PAGES 12-13 Country life: p12 t © Still life, from the Praedia of Julia Felix, Pompeii (wall painting), Roman / Museo Archeologico Nazionale, Naples, Italy / © Samuel Magal, Sites & Photos Ltd. / Bridgeman Images; p12 bl © Iberfoto / Iberfoto / Superstock; p12 br © akg-images / De Agostini Picture Lib. / G. Dagli Orti; p13 t © DeAgostini / DeAgostini / Superstock; p13 l © Bottle with two handles, Imperial Period (glass), Roman, (1st century AD) / Museum of Fine Arts, Boston, Massachusetts, USA / Henry Lillie Pierce Fund / Bridgeman Images; p13 mr © Mimmo Jodice/Corbis; p13 b © Ribbed Bowl, Early Imperial Period, late 1st century BC-1st century AD (mosaic glass), Roman / Museum of Fine Arts, Boston, Massachusetts, USA / Henry Lillie Pierce Fund / Bridgeman Images.

PAGES 14-15 Growing up: p14 t © DeAgostini / DeAgostini / Superstock; p14 ml © Ancient Art & Architecture Collection Ltd / Alamy; p14 m © The Trustees of the British Museum; p14 mr © DeAgostini / DeAgostini / Superstock; p15 tl © Heritage Image Partnership Ltd / Alamy; p15 tr © The Art Archive / Alamy; p15 b © The Trustees of the British Museum.

PAGES 16-17 Fashion and beauty: p16 t © DeAgostini / DeAgostini / Superstock; p16 bl © Woman Pouring Perfume into a Phial (fresco), Roman, (1st century AD) / Museo Nazionale, Rome, Italy / Giraudon / Bridgeman Images; p16 br © PhotoStock-Israel / Alamy; p17 tr © Bettmann/CORBIS; p17 m © The Trustees of the British Museum; p17 bl © World History Archive / Alamy; p17 bm © The Trustees of the British Museum; p17 br © The Art Archive / Alamy.

PAGES 18-19 At the games: p18 bl © Iberfoto / Iberfoto / Superstock; p18 mr © The Art Archive / Archaeological Museum Naples / Araldo De Luca; p18 br © Gary Ombler / Dorling Kindersley / Getty Images; p19 t © Battle of gladiators against the wildcats, detail depicting a gladiator running through a wildcat, 320 AD (mosaic), Roman, (4th century AD) / Galleria Borghese, Rome, Italy / Alinari / Bridgeman Images; p19 m © De Agostini Picture Library / Getty Images; p19 b © The Trustees of the British Museum.

PAGES 20-21 Entertainment: p20 tr © Photo Scala, Florence/Fotografica Foglia - courtesy of the Ministero Beni e Att. Culturali; p20 ml © The Art Archive / DeA Picture Library / G. Nimatallah; p20 br © Peter Horree / Alamy; p21 t © The Art Archive / Alamy; p21 m and bl © Museum of London.

PAGES 24-25 Pompeii: p24 ml © Michael Kemp / Alamy; p24 mr © Robert Harding Picture Library Ltd / Alamy; p24 br © Riot at the amphitheater, detail, from Italy, Campania, Pompeii, painting on plaster, 55-79 B.C. / De Agostini Picture Library / Bridgeman Images; p25 t © akg-images / Mondadori Portfolio / Luciano Pedicini; p25 m © The Art Archive / Alamy; p25 ml © Small clay bowl containing red powder for frescoes, artifact uncovered in Pompeii, Campania, Italy, Roman Civilization, 1st century / Museo Archeologico Nazionale, Naples, Italy / De Agostini Picture Library / L. Pedicini / Bridgeman Images; p25 ml © Small clay bowl containing purple powder for frescoes, artifact uncovered in Pompeii, Campania, Italy, Roman Civilization, 1st century / Museo Archeologico Nazionale, Naples, Italy / De Agostini Picture Library / L. Pedicini / Bridgeman Images; p25 mr © akg-images / Erich Lessing.

PAGES 26-27 Master builders: p26 t © Robert Harding Picture Library Ltd / Alamy; p27 tr © ACTIVE MUSEUM / Alamy.

PAGES 28-29 The fall of Rome: p28 ml © Photo Scala, Florence; p28 br © B.O'Kane / Alamy; p29 tl © World History Archive / Topfoto; p29 m © Photo Scala, Florence; p29 br © Album / Oronoz / Album / Superstock.

Additional design by Stephen Moncrieff and Lenka Hrehova

Digital Manipulation by John Russell   With thanks to Ruth King